# WINE *lover*

Ed Foster

summersdale

WINE LOVER

Illustrations by Kath Walker

Summersdale Publishers Ltd
46 West Street
Chichester
West Sussex
PO19 1RP
UK

www.summersdale.com

Printed and bound in China

ISBN: 978-1-84953-124-5

Substantial discounts on bulk quantities of Summersdale books are available to corporations, professional associations and other organisations. For details contact Summersdale Publishers by telephone: +44 (0) 1243 771107, fax: +44 (0) 1243 786300 or email: nicky@summersdale.com.

To: ...........................................................

From: .........................................................

It is well to remember that there are
five reasons for drinking: the arrival of
a friend; one's present or future thirst;
the excellence of the wine;
or any other reason.

Latin proverb

Here's to the corkscrew – a useful key
to unlock the storehouse of wit, the
treasury of laughter, the front door
of fellowship and the gate
of pleasant folly!

W. E. P. French

My idea of a fine wine was one that merely stained my teeth without stripping the enamel.

Clive James, *Falling Towards England*

The soil of the famous Clos de Vougeot (a vineyard in the Burgundy district of France) is considered so precious that the workers are required to scrape their shoes before they leave.

Wine is a living liquid containing

no preservatives.

Julia Child

The soft extractive note of an aged cork being withdrawn has the true sound of a man opening his heart.

William S. Benwell, *Journey to Wine in Victoria*

I was planning to expand my horizons,
seek happiness and harmony in
nature, and find a new sense of
'belongingness'... And, if all that failed,
I told myself, I could always seek
happiness in an excellent
supply of red wine.

Karen Wheeler, *Tout Sweet*

The labels on jars of wine uncovered from Tutankhamen's tomb were so detailed that they would comply with today's wine label laws. They included information on the year that the wines were corked and the grower, as well as additional comments regarding quality.

Burgundy makes you think of silly
things, Bordeaux makes you talk
of them and champagne
makes you do them.

Jean Anthelme Brillat-Savarin

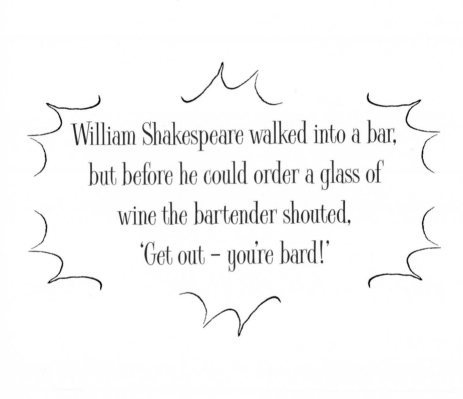

William Shakespeare walked into a bar, but before he could order a glass of wine the bartender shouted, 'Get out – you're bard!'

Mrs Jennings in Jane Austen's *Sense and Sensibility* recommends South Africa's famous Constantia wine for lovelorn heroines because of its 'healing powers on a disappointed heart'.

Wine... the intellectual part of the meal.

Alexandre Dumas

I never touch it – unless I'm thirsty.

Lily Bollinger on champagne

Corton-Charlemagne, a well-known white burgundy, is said to have been created after the wife of the eighth-century Frankish Emperor Charlemagne demonstrated such a contempt for red wine stains on her husband's beard that it prompted him to order white vines be planted.

- Will you join me in a glass of wine?
- You get in first, and if there's
room enough, I'll join you.

Neil Brant, *International House*

The word 'plonk', often used to describe cheap wine, was first coined in Australia in the early twentieth century. It is believed by some to have derived from the French *vin blanc* that Australian soldiers brought back after World War One, while another interpretation is that the name comes from the sound of a cork being extracted from a bottle.

Good wine is a good familiar
creature if it be well used.

William Shakespeare, *Othello*

# I am tasting stars!

Dom Pérignon on his first sip of champagne

Let us have wine and women,
mirth and laughter,
Sermons and soda water the day after.

Lord Byron, *Don Juan*

I drink when I have occasion, and
sometimes when I have no occasion.

Cervantes

A particularly stomach-churning hangover cure in Roman times was deep-fried canaries, whilst the ancient Greeks preferred to soak up last night's plonk with a plate of sheep's lung. Rabbit-dropping tea was a cure favoured by cowboys of the Old Wild West.

'Hock' is the nickname coined by Queen Victoria for wines produced in the Hochheim region of Germany.

I spent ninety percent of my money on wine, women and song and just wasted the other ten percent.

Ronnie Hawkins

What though youth gave love and roses,
Age still leaves us friends and wine.

Thomas Moore, 'Spring and Autumn'

The longest recorded champagne cork flight
was 177 feet and 9 inches, 4 feet from
level ground at Woodbury Vineyards
in New York State.

# Wine is bottled poetry.

Robert Louis Stevenson

According to John Betjeman, Oscar Wilde
'sipped at a weak hock and seltzer as he gazed
at the London skies' while awaiting his arrest
at the Cadogan Hotel in 1895.

In victory you deserve champagne,
in defeat you need it.

Napoleon Bonaparte

Wine, taken in moderation, makes life,
for a moment, better, and when the
moment passes life does not for
that reason become worse.

Bernard Levin, *From the Camargue to the Alps*

A New Zealand variety of Sauvignon Blanc was officially renamed 'Cat's Pee on a Gooseberry Bush' after Oz Clarke coined the phrase on first tasting it. Surprisingly, it has sold well throughout the world, but US authorities have since insisted that it be renamed 'Cat's Phee on a Gooseberry Bush.'

Persian mythology states that an unnamed
woman discovered wine after drinking from a
jar of fermented grape juice, and woke up
from sleep cured of a headache.

What contemptible scoundrel stole
the cork from my lunch?

W. C. Fields

I'm like old wine. They don't bring me out very often, but I'm well preserved.

Rose F. Kennedy

It is unknown who made the first corkscrew, but the very first man to patent a corkscrew design was Samuel Henshall, in 1795. The design, an early version of today's popular twisting pull corkscrew, was said to have been inspired by a device used to extract bullets from wounds.

I told my wife that a husband is like a fine wine; he gets better with age. The next day, she locked me in the cellar.

When I read about the evils of
drinking, I gave up reading.

Henny Youngman

The drips of wine left on the inside of a glass
after it has been swirled are often called 'legs'.
They are also known as 'tears',
or even 'church windows'.

The sharper is the berry,
the sweeter is the wine.

Proverb

Champagne is the only wine that leaves
a woman beautiful after drinking it.

Madame de Pompadour

Richard Nixon would cover his wine labels with napkins so as to hide his preference for French wine rather than one from his own country.

Quickly, bring me a beaker of wine,
so that I may wet my mind and say
something clever.

Aristophanes

If you are as passionate about Pachelbel as you are Pinot Noir, you may be interested to learn that one South African vineyard constantly pipes baroque music to its grapes – apparently the vines appear to be visibly healthier as a result.

Wine comes in at the mouth
And love comes in at the eye;
That's all we shall know for truth
Before we grow old and die.

William Butler Yeats, 'A Drinking Song'

The Romans used lead as a preservative for wine, they also discovered that it gave it a pleasant sweet taste, but the poisonous effects are believed to have contributed to the Roman Empire's eventual decline.

'*Más vino* – you must drink more wine,' announced the waiter, flamboyantly replenishing my glass with the José Ferrer. 'You must drink *mucho, mucho vino* with the snails, señor. It is the Mallorcan custom. The *All-i-oli* purifies the souls of the *caracoles* and the *vino* sends them to heaven happy. *Más vino!*'

Peter Kerr, *Snowball Oranges*

Penicillin cures but wine
makes people happy.

Sir Alexander Fleming

I find friendship to be like wine, raw
when new, ripened with age, the true
old man's milk and restorative cordial.

Thomas Jefferson

The two-pronged corkscrew is the only
corkscrew that does not make a hole in the
cork. Two prongs, one longer than the other, are
positioned either side of the cork within the
bottle. With a slight twist and pull,
the cork is released.

My only regret is that I did
not drink more champagne.

Lord Maynard Keynes on his deathbed

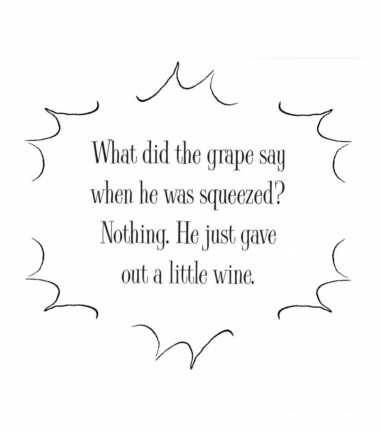

What did the grape say
when he was squeezed?
Nothing. He just gave
out a little wine.

The most expensive bottle of wine ever sold was a 1787 Château Lafite, which was sold for a cool £105,000 at Christie's London in 1985. It once belonged to Thomas Jefferson.

I had never cared about lunch, until
I was introduced to Sunday ones in
Tuscan vineyards. Celebrations of food
and wine amongst friends and family,
they transcend the notion of mere meals
and transform into a theatre
for the senses.

Victoria Cosford, *Amore and Amaretti*

Wine – very nice. I wonder how they got the cat to sit on the bottle?

Stephen Fry, *The Liar*

'Fining' is a process involving the removal of compounds such as copper ions from a wine to improve its flavour. Milk, Irish moss and even bull's blood have been used as fining agents in the past, though egg whites, isinglass (a form of collagen from the dried swim bladders of fish) and gelatine are more commonly used today. These fining agents are not present in the wine once it is corked, but if the wine label says 'suitable for vegetarians or vegans' it is referring to what has been used during the fining process.

Sorrow can be alleviated by good sleep,
a bath and a glass of wine.

St Thomas Aquinas

Champagne! I love it. It tastes
like your foot's asleep.

Jack Yellen, *George White's Scandals*

Wine makes every meal an occasion,
every table more elegant,
every day more civilised.

André Simon, *Commonsense of Wine*

I have enjoyed great health at a great age because every day since I can remember I have consumed a bottle of wine except when I have not felt well. Then I have consumed two bottles.

Attributed to the Bishop of Seville

A popular Haitian myth claims that sticking 13 pins in the cork of the bottle during the time of consumption will ward off a hangover. Inhaling smoke from a coal fire and rubbing limes on your body prior to a night's drinking are other strange preventative measures touted around the globe.

'Sack' is an old-fashioned term for the fortified wines that were produced in Spain and the Canary Islands during the sixteenth century. It's the drink of choice for Falstaff, the roly-poly drunkard who appears in several of Shakespeare's plays, and most closely resembles cheap sherry consumed today.

Wine is the most healthful and
most hygienic of beverages.

Louis Pasteur

When it came to drinking laws, ancient Greek philosopher Plato had similar ideas to those of modern Britain, believing that the minimum drinking age should be 18. However, he also said that wine should be drunk in moderation until you are 30, and you should wait for 40 to drink as much as you like to temper the 'crabbedness of old age'.

For when the wine is in, the wit is out.

Thomas Becon, *Catechism*

He's such a connoisseur. He not only knows the year the wine was made but he can tell you who stamped on the grapes.

Edith Gwynn

The writer should never like a wine, he
should be in love with it; never find a
wine disappointing but identify
it as a mortal enemy, an
attempt to poison him.

Auberon Waugh, *Waugh on Wine*

There are approximately forty-four million bubbles in a bottle of champagne, and the pressure inside the bottle is equivalent to three times that of the pressure inside an average car tyre.

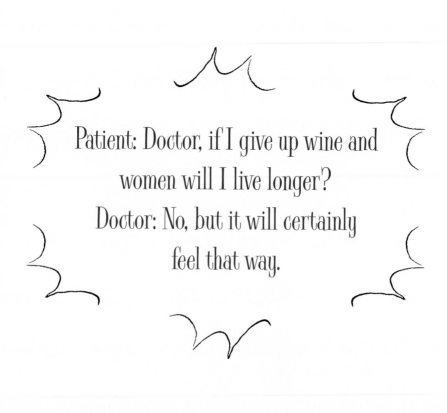

Patient: Doctor, if I give up wine and women will I live longer?
Doctor: No, but it will certainly feel that way.

Too much Chablis can
make you whablis.

Ogden Nash

Drink wine, and you will sleep well.
Sleep, and you will not sin. Avoid sin,
and you will be saved. Ergo,
drink wine and be saved.

Medieval German proverb

Wine is the most civilised
thing in the world.

Ernest Hemingway

www.summersdale.com